kent HUMPHREYS

SHEPHERDING HORSES

Understanding God's Plan for Transforming Leaders

DiaKonia

SHEPHERDING HORSES
Understanding God's Plan For Transforming Leaders
published by Diakonia Publishing

Copyright © 2008 by Kent Humphreys
ISBN: 978-0-9800877-1-0

Unless otherwise noted, Scripture quotations are from *the HOLY BIBLE, NEW INTERNATIONAL VERSION*. Copyright © 1973, 1978, 1984 by International Bible Society. Used by permission of Zondervan Publishing House. All rights reserved.

Scripture references and quotations marked (New American Standard) were taken from the *New American Standard Bible* © 1995 Lockman Foundation.

Scripture references and quotations marked (Phillips) were taken from *The New Testament in Modern English*, John Bertram Phillips; London: G. Bles, © 1958.

Scripture references and quotations marked (Living) were taken from *The Living Bible, Paraphrased,*. Kenneth N. Taylor, Wheaton, Illinois: Tyndale House Publishers, © 1971.

No part of this publication may be reproduced, stored in a retrieval system, or transmitted, in any form or by any means—electronic, mechanical, photocopying, recording or otherwise—without prior written permission.

For information:
DIAKONIA PUBLISHING
P.O. Box 9512
Greensboro, NC 27429
www.ephesians412.net

table of contents

Foreword V

Chapter One

Shepherding Horses 1

Chapter Two

What Did Jesus Do? 19

Chapter Three

Building Bridges Between
Pastors and Workplace Leaders 33

Conclusion 51

How May We Help You? 52

Other Resources
By Kent Humphreys 53

*Scripture is taken from the New International Version
unless otherwise indicated in the text*

I

Dear Reader,

You cannot imagine the encouragement it was to receive this e-mail following a speaking engagement in Singapore, during which I shared the contents of this book to seven hundred pastors and church leaders from seventeen countries. Responses such as this one gave me the motivation to pursue God's prompting in my spirit to put these ideas in writing. This book is the result of that effort, and I pray that the contents will both challenge and encourage your heart to understand, equip, and send the community leaders in your congregation to do the work of the church out in the world in which they live and work. I pray that your own heart, your church, and your city will never be the same.

God Bless His Church and
His ministry through you,

Kent Humphreys

"DO YOU GIVE THE
HORSE
HIS STRENGTH, OR

CLOTHE
HIS NECK WITH A
FLOWING MANE?"

Job 39:19

foreword

It seems that every pastor begins his vocational ministry with his cross hairs aimed at growing his church, and I was no exception. Like most pastors, I went to many "church growth" seminars and conferences, with the honest intent of growing our church. The idea, in short, being to try to get people on the outside to come inside and be "one of us", isolating them from the outside as much as possible. Now, after twelve years at the church I now serve as pastor, God has done a work in my heart to understand that the work of the church is not just the programs that occur inside the buildings of the local congregation, but the ministries that God gives the church members out in their worlds of work and community.

Jesus said, *"I will build my church"*, so the burden is off of me to do that. In fact, church growth can be the best way to limit Kingdom growth for our Lord. That is like saying to your best sales reps, "keep the store stocked well so when they come through the doors we can sell them our product". The problem is that unchurched people are not "charging the doors" of the church for a deal. I've learned that you can not get a harvest without planting the seeds. Our communities and work places aren't seeded very well, and the result is that very little growth is taking place in most churches. Our culture is fast becoming more secular because the American church particularly has become "ingrown".

The fact is, Jesus trained, equipped, encouraged, and then left the best sales reps (his horses) in charge of the store...to do one thing...take the gospel **out** to where the people were, to live it, demonstrate it and expect a harvest. From that He would "build His church".

So what practical steps can we as "pastor leaders" take to model what Jesus did, equipping and encouraging our workplace leaders to demonstrate this same "GOOD NEWS" to our world outside? How do I, as a pastor, equip the *"sheep"* (most of the congregation) and encourage the *"horses"* (that small group of leaders within each congregation) to focus on their part of the Kingdom and let Jesus build His church? Kent

Humphreys has made this seemingly difficult process into an understandable and workable one.

It has been with great anticipation that I have waited for a book like this one to be available to myself and other pastors, a book that is filled with not only Biblical principles, but practical steps explaining how to understand, have a relationship with, and equip the business and community leaders in our congregations.

I have been Kent's pastor for twelve years, and I can attest to the fact that Kent lives what he teaches, and that he has blessed thousands of pastors with his heart to help them understand "horses" like himself. He is definitely a "horse" in my congregation that understands his ministry out in his sphere of influence, and who enriches, strengthens and enlarges our congregation because of it.

Pastors, there are a lot more of them than there are of us. Train them and send them out!
And be ready for your church to grow!

Pastor Ray Ivey
Cherokee Hills Baptist Church
Oklahoma City, Oklahoma

chapter one

SHEPHERDING HORSES

THE ALLEGORY

I would like to take the liberty of writing this book as if we were having a conversation, you, the readers, and me. I would further like permission to use both allegory and image to paint a mental picture. The picture is that of a shepherd, tending his herd of sheep, into which some wild horses have infiltrated. In our allegory, the shepherd is the pastor, the sheep are most of the members of his congregation, and the horses are the strong workplace leaders within the church. They may or may not be leaders in the organization of their church, but they are leaders in their sphere of influence outside of the church.

Let me make very clear who these horses are amongst your flock. By strong leaders I do not intend to convey that every leader fits into this category. These "horses" are the small minority of men and women, who, by their nature, are naturally dominant individuals. They are often found as owners or CEOs in business, and often leaders in the community, perhaps even politically. They love to start things, and one of their most visible characteristics is a desire to control. If they are in a group, they want to be in charge. The way they exhibit such behavior in a church setting is that they avoid most programs when they are not in charge. They will acquiesce to a leader with more authority, so they will sit under your preaching, and they may be chairman of the personnel or finance committee (areas where they feel comfortable to exert control and leadership), but they will probably show little support for other programs and functions in the church. These are not just leaders; they are strong, confident, intimidating type "A" leaders.

There are other leaders in your church, of course, but they are not as wild as these horses. Your flock is full of leadership of all types, but for the purpose of our allegory, everyone who isn't one of these "wild horses", we are calling "sheep". Neither is better than the other; they are just different. The purpose of this book is to help you, Pastor, understand these wild ones, and learn to train them to come under God's control and become the ministers in their world that God intends for them to be. You see, the "sheep" are characterized by a desire to fit in – to be part of the family. They are happy to sit under your preaching; they even pay attention and try to apply the principles to their lives. When it is time to sign up for small group Bible Studies, they do. They come, participate, and benefit. Although all members of your church need to be taught and discipled (trained), the "sheep" just seem easier to reach than the wild horses.

After reading this far, you may be asking yourself why it is important for you to understand or work with such a small group within your church. There are at least two reasons. First, they simply cannot be trained using methods that work for most, so methods must be used that work for them. Secondly, these individuals have key positions of influence and leadership in the community, in their marketplaces, and in their churches. Your mission is to train them to use that influence for godly purposes, to reach the people in such places for the Lord. The horses need to realize that their positions are actually places of ministry, not just platforms for their own gain, and you are the one to guide them.

Some of you, Readers, are shepherd pastors. You may have been to seminary, where you were given much instruction as to the care, guidance, protection, and feeding of sheep. You have since been awakened to the fact that the seminary did little if any preparation for you in the training of horses. They are wild stallions and mares of all shapes and varieties, who tend to snort, paw the ground, sometimes cause chaos, and generally do not listen or react in a quiet compliant manner. What are you to do with them?

Some of you, Readers, are horses. You are a leader by personality, by background, and by experience. When you attend church with the sheep, you feel awkward, as if you do not quite fit in. You may have a leadership position in the church, but your passion is probably aimed at what you do outside of the church walls.

A few of you, Readers, are sheep. (I say a few because this book was written primarily to Pastors, but a few of you sheep may be peeking in.) You are a loyal member in the church, you support the Pastor, and you follow his shepherding; but you may wonder at times about those horses because of the wild things they do and the chaos they can create.

Some of you are sheep, some of you are shepherds, some of you are horses, and a few of you are a combination. I have a friend, Shawn, who is from Beijing, China. Shawn is both a shepherd and a horse. He leads a house church in Beijing, and he is also a business leader. He represents a whole new category of shepherd horses around the world. Let's look more specifically at shepherding horses.

THE HORSES

Almost every summer my extended family makes a trip to Colorado to ride horses at a ranch hidden in a beautiful valley, nestled in the spectacular Rocky Mountains. During that week, each of us learns to know the unique personality of our horse. Their names are as varied as their riders. It seems fitting when Davidene, my wife, gets to ride "Calamity Jane" or when I ride "Bid Daddy". The pre-school aged grandchildren always get led around on the elderly chestnut mare "Flicka", or the stately, if ancient, white gentleman, "Borax". It is an adventure for all.

We have learned over the years that the key to having fun, whether loping up trails or walking through trees, is control. When the rider has the horse under control, it is a good experience. The wranglers tell the guests that speed is not the important thing; control is paramount to everything else. For a "dude", who rides for only one week a year, this can be an interesting challenge. Some of the guests are expert riders, but even they can have problems if a horse exerts his independence, or spooks and bolts unexpectedly. We are constantly reminded that horses are powerful, and the rider must remain in control regardless of how small he is compared to this magnificent animal.

With that scene as the backdrop to our thoughts, let's shift to the image of the pastor shepherd and his congregation flock. It is true that ALL of us are like sheep (Isaiah 53) and have gone our own rebellious way. God has laid all of our sin upon His Son, the perfect lamb of sacrifice. In that sense, all of us are like sheep who are in desperate need of a shepherd and savior. In our analogy, most sheep in the flock will follow the shepherd. The pastor may have to care for them, guide them, and rescue them constantly, but they will respond to him. However, as a shepherd, he has a dual responsibility to train his horses concurrently with leading his sheep. It is not a choice. If he ignores them, the horses will still be there, depositing manure on the floor of the church (horses are messy individuals). But remember, there is great blessing in training them. If they are trained, horses will multiply the ministry of the church and of God's work in the marketplace and community. Let's now look at what it takes to train a horse.

THE TRAINING

My nephew, Zac Parrington of Topeka, Kansas, trains horses. He has been doing this since he was a young kid. Not only does he train his own, which he uses in rodeo events, but he also trains four to six horses at a time for other people. I asked Zac to share with me the key steps he uses in training the horses. He shared with me the simple process that takes him only thirty days to complete.

1. *The first step involves earning the trust of the horse. Zac says that the goal is to make the horse want to do the things you desire for him to do. You must convince him that you have his best interest at heart. How is that done? The initial step involves slow and quiet approach, quiet talking and touching, and getting very close to the horse. Let him see in your eyes, and you look into his. He will SEE and experience that he can trust. You do not make quick or sudden moves at this point, because he is cautious and can be fearful. He quiets down and begins to pay attention to what you want as he learns that you are not there to hurt him.*

   What does this process look like with a pastor and a workplace leader? First, Pastor, approach him or her without an agenda except to get to know him. Ask him out to lunch. He may fall down out of complete surprise, and when he picks himself up, he will probably be suspicious that you either want money, or want him to take a job in a church program. Assure him that is not the case. He may worry about why you want to see him one on one, but that worry will be quickly dissolved. Meet him at his place of work, not at yours, and take him to eat. While there, ask about himself and his work. Get to know him, how he thinks, what he likes to do, and what his aspirations are. Show interest with questions about him and his family. Do not bring up the church or its programs. If he asks about them, answer his question quickly and get off the subject. This will convince him that your agenda really is just to get to know him better. An ability to trust in this relationship will have been started.

2. The second step is to let the horse think that "getting under control" with a bridle and a saddle is a good idea. You want to be firm, but you must allow room for the horse to think for himself. While he thinks he wants to be free to roam the pastures and hills, you want to make him a roping horse. You must convince the horse that training for a new goal (roping) is good for him, so that it becomes HIS choice.

> Does this sound like an impossible task with the horses of your congregation? Without God's intervention, it certainly is. But as you spend time with a leader, allowing him to get close to your life (which he is now watching closely) you will have the opportunity to model how God intends for us to do life. The "horse" will get to know you on a deeper level, willing to listen as you teach him God's ways. He will learn what it means to walk and live daily with God, and the Holy Spirit will become the bridle and bit that controls and moves him.

3. Finally, the trainer must prepare him for the distractions of life. Zac rides the horse next to cars, close to wildlife, and takes him for a ride in a trailer. He is patient and gives these exercises plenty of time. The objective is to get the horse to stay focused, even when there are distractions.

> Pastor, this is such an important lesson for your horses. They live in a world of distractions that would pull them from God's way. While your 'business', the church, is run from a Biblical perspective, theirs usually is not. Their world is chaotic, filled with temptations and people who are fearful and angry. How can they walk in such a world, touching these

very people with God's love, and not lose their focus on God? Train them by coming along side them in their world, helping them to see the "cars" that could hit them, the wildlife that would corrupt them, and God's pathway for their lives. Be there with them, experiencing with them, patiently and firmly showing them a new way. (We will cover many practical ways to do this later in the book.)

In just thirty days, Zac is able to earn a horse's trust, get him under control, and prepare him to keep his focus even when distracted. It is a sobering thought that a trainer like Zac spends more "one on one" time training a horse in thirty days, than most pastors spend training a next generation leader over a period of years. Training takes time and individual attention, but is well worth it. It is exactly what Jesus did with His "horses".

The horse is the best example I can think of in trying to explain to you, a pastor, how leaders in the workplace think and respond. (As an entrepreneur CEO, I count myself among the horses.) By their personality, talent, gifting, background, and opportunities, they have been given great strength by God. However, this strength can be used for either good or evil. We horses live in a different world than you do, and have unique opportunities to multiply our influence; but we desperately need training and direction from our shepherds.

In God's Word we see which characteristics God uses when referring to horses. These characteristics will be the ones that you encounter while you are training your horses.

THE HORSES' CHARACTER

They Are Self-Sufficient

In Deuteronomy 17:16, the Bible says that the King of Israel *"must not acquire great numbers of horses for himself or make the people to return to Egypt to get more of them, for the Lord has told you, 'You are not to go that way again.'"* Horses were a symbol of strength, and Egypt symbolized past life. God's people were not to depend on their own strength, but God's, and they were not to go back to their old life. Workplace leaders easily rely on their own strength instead of depending on God.

The trouble with leaders like me is that we are not dependent upon Christ, so we have to be broken. We need for you, as a pastor, to help us understand the brokenness process and learn from it. We are exposed to the pitfalls of power and lust and greed and success. If the honest truth be told, pastors have helped us remain self-sufficient and independent by allowing us to be comfortable giving money to the church without becoming disciples. The churches have allowed leaders who are successful in the marketplace to be exempt from the rules that limit other people because they have wealth, power, and influence. You, as a pastor, are often intimidated by that leader. What you don't know is that he is intimidated by you. He thinks that you are a spiritual person and that he is not. The situation exists, then, that the workplace leader is intimidated by the pastor and the pastor is intimidated by the workplace leader and the only place they get together is on the budget committee. The relationship you forge with this leader will bridge this gap for both of you.

They Are Affected By A Pagan Marketplace

2 Kings 23:11-12 *"He did away with the horses which the kings of Judah had given to the sun,… and he burned the chariots of the sun with fire."*

In 2 Kings the story is written of King Josiah cleansing the Temple. During the process, the horses were removed because they had been dedicated to the sun god. Horses were often used in pagan worship practices. This passage could remind us that many of your congregation must work in the pagan marketplace, one that does not follow the One True God.

Some of the horses in your congregations have become unholy and blemished because of their decisions made while working in a pagan environment, and some pastors shy away from them because of it. Those pastors want to stay just close enough to be able to "pastor" them, but not too close. The result is that, in some cases, the most unholy and needy people in the church do not get the same attention as the sheep, because regardless of how dirty the sheep are, they are easier to work with than the rebellious horses that the pastor does not understand.

They Are Strong And Fearless In Battle

God used horses as part of His answer to Job in Job 39:19-25. *"Do you give the horse his strength, or clothe his neck with a flowing mane? Do you make him leap like a locust, striking terror with his proud snorting? He paws fiercely, rejoicing in his strength, and charges into the fray. He laughs at fear, afraid of nothing; he does not shy away from the sword. The quiver rattles against his side, along with the flashing spear and lance. In frenzied excitement he eats up the ground; he cannot stand still when the trumpet sounds. At the blast of the trumpet he snorts, 'Aha!' He catches the scent of battle from afar, the shout of commanders and the battle cry…"*

God gives the horse his strength. The horse has great leaping ability and takes pride in his strength, just as the marketplace leaders who attend your church do. They have been carefully trained by years in the workplace to not show fear. The horse does not "shy away from the sword" of battle, and neither do the leaders. In fact, many of them thrive on it; they love the thrill of combat. These leaders enter the fray just as the horse does in "frenzied excitement". They, too, "cannot stand still". You probably already have some names popping into your mind as you think about the horses in your church, don't you?

It is only God who can turn an individual with an independent, stubborn, fearless spirit into one who is submissive, humble, and controlled by the "bit" of the Holy Spirit to do God's will and work in his world; however, God has chosen to use you as His change agent in many such lives. You are the gentle trainer who will help to bend this horse's heart to seek God in his life. A great Biblical example of this principle is seen in the life of Paul.

Of all of the horses in the Bible, Paul was among the wildest. He was strong in personality, passionate in his actions, couldn't keep still for a moment, was driven and intense, supremely confident in himself, and could not wait to get into battle! But God, the Almighty Shepherd, saw his heart. Saul was driven by a desire for justice and right. He truly believed, as a Roman, that Christians were a genuine threat to his beloved Rome. So he went out to kill them, to do his best to get rid of the threat. What happened next is an eternal example that God will do whatever it takes to get a man's attention and turn his heart toward Him.

God met him on the road to Damascus. In a blaze of light and glory, God forced Saul to see Him and to know who He was, and Saul became Paul, a forever changed man. Only God can do this in someone's heart. The moment of conversion is always between God and an individual. But even this wild stallion needed to be broken and humbled, and God uses other people to accomplish that work. In Paul's case, God had to keep Paul slowed down (probably the only slow time in his life), and he did this by allowing him to remain blind for a time. Paul may have thought that this was a catastrophe, a common way for us to view crises, but God knew that it was the beginning of the best part of Paul's life.

During this time, God brought a man, Ananias, to train this horse. Now Ananias wasn't too sure that he wanted the job; after all, "Saul" was on a mission to kill men such as him! But Ananias trusted that God would lead him one step at a time and show him what to do. (You may feel the same way with your horses, but God is faithful to guide the process if you are willing.) During this time, Paul learned how to have a personal relationship with God, and became a lover of God and of people.

Paul, of course, retained his horse-like traits throughout his life, but he was now a horse submissive to God and used mightily of Him. As one of God's shepherds, watch for these stallions and be ready to move along side of them to train them when God has made them ready. God will tell you which ones are ready, just as He told Ananias, and you can trust Him to guide you as you go.

They Create False Hopes

Psalms 33:17 teaches us that in spite of the great strength of the horse, it cannot always accomplish what we hope. "*A horse is a vain hope for deliverance; despite all its great strength it cannot save.*"

We in the workplace, we who are leaders, have so often given false hopes to our spouses, to our children, to our co-workers, to our pastors and to our church families. Out in our daily experiences between Sundays, people are constantly treating us as though we are important and valuable. We hear regularly what a good job we are doing. We feel strong, capable in ourselves, invincible. Praise directed to us breeds pride, and that pride easily carries over into spiritual pride as well. Every leader in the workplace must constantly learn the lesson that it is not our own strength that can accomplish true success or righteousness.

When our eyes are on the Lord and sensitive to His guidance, He can use our great strength in concert with His wishes. But when we feel that we can do things alone, without His direction, we fail and must come humbly back to Him.

They Represent Man's Effort Instead Of God's Provision

Isaiah 31:1 "*Woe to those who go down to Egypt for help and rely on horses, and trust in chariots because they are many, and in horsemen because they are very strong, But they do not look to the Holy One of Israel, nor seek the Lord!*"

There is a constant struggle that workplace leaders face. They are to be in the world, but not of it. They want to impact their culture, but not become like it. They must understand their gifts and talents, but not rely on them instead of on God. These talents and gifts are to be used for His glory alone. Their stubborn will must be broken, just like a horse's. Then they must daily submit to the guidance of the Holy Spirit. Finally, they must depend only on God's strength, not their own.

You see, we, as horses, need a lot of help. We are in trouble and out of control, and most of us do not even know it, (although we suspect it due to the stresses of our lives).

Jeremiah 8:6-7 says, "*No man repented of his wickedness, saying, 'What have I done?'*

Everyone turned to his course, like a horse charging into the battle. But my people do not know the ordinance of the Lord."

You, as a pastor/shepherd/horse trainer have been called to shepherd these stubborn horses. You have been called to train them to voluntarily submit to the guidance of the Holy Spirit. Only the Living God can equip you to this task, but He is able and ready to do just that. It is His work, and He will accomplish it – through you if you so choose.

One final thought:

When you get a few leaders trained and you allow them to use their gifts and abilities as leaders, then they will help you care for and equip the rest of the sheep and your schedule will become sensible. If you will give part of your life to a few horses, you will see them fulfilling their responsibilities in the church, in the community, and in the workplace. Then, while you are doing what God has called you to do, (to pastor, to teach, to equip), they will be helping you.

QUESTIONS

1. Are you spending most of your time with the sheep, or have you set aside some time for training and equipping the horses?

2. Which of the leaders (horses) in your church has recently been broken (by circumstances allowed by God), and now appears ready for some personalized training?

You see, what we, as horses, consider as adversity when we lose business, finances, our health, or other things, can be used by God to break and humble us. That is the kind of horse in whom you want to invest. You do not want to look just for the horse with the strongest personality, because he may not want God right now. The wealthiest one may not feel like he needs God. Wait for that person to have a crisis in his life and then build bridges of relationship with him or her.

3. Which leaders in your church appear to "have it all together", yet are still in need of a trainer?

They may be waiting for you to help them to go to the next level in their walk with God.

4. Are you willing to be a horse trainer?

It takes time, and it means making some decisions about how you use your time. A pastor with whom I recently had lunch said, "Kent, if I am going to be more of a horse trainer, it means I have got to stop doing some things in my present ministry to make the time." I replied, "Yes, Pastor, and one of the most difficult things about that is telling your congregation that you don't do those things any more. It changes your job description, and change frightens people. But you have to decide, 'Who is going to set my job description?' Let doing what Jesus did in His ministry be your example of how to pattern yours." In the next chapter, we will do exactly that – look at the things Jesus did to train horses as he shepherded sheep.

"DO YOU MAKE HIM LEAP LIKE A LOCUST, **STRIKING** TERROR WITH HIS PROUD SNORTING?

HE PAWS FIERCELY, **REJOICING** IN HIS STRENGTH, AND CHARGES INTO THE FRAY. HE LAUGHS AT FEAR, AFRAID OF **NOTHING.**"

Job 39:20-22a

chapter two

WHAT DID JESUS DO?

Jesus was, of course, the perfect shepherd, the Good Shepherd, who laid down His life for the sheep. He had perfect love, perfect purpose, and a perfect method to train His horses. If we follow His method, we will have God's blessing for success. Jesus did five things:

1. He told everyone to respond to the Good News
2. He taught many to understand God's principles
3. He trained some to do the work
4. He equipped a few to reproduce
5. He modeled a relationship with the Father

Let's look at these closely.

Jesus Told Everyone To Respond To The Good News

Mark 1:14-15 *"Jesus came into Galilee proclaiming the Gospel of God, saying, 'The time has come at last – the Kingdom of God has arrived. You must change your hearts and believe the good news.'"* (Phillips)

Mark 1:18 *"At once, they dropped their nets and followed Him."* (Phillips)

Mark 16:15 *"You must go out to the whole world and proclaim the Gospel to every creature."* (Phillips)

Whenever Jesus came into a community, He told everyone the good news, and that is why people immediately surrounded Him. We, as a church today, are doing a good job of sharing the good news of Jesus Christ through evangelism, church services, videos, newspapers, radio, television, internet, magazines, tracts, and so forth. Jesus told everyone.

Jesus Taught Many To Understand God's Principles

Mark 12:38 *"The vast crowd heard this with great delight, and Jesus continued His teaching."* (Phillips)

Mark 7:14-15 *"Listen to Me, all of you, and understand."* (New American Standard)

Mark 7:18 *"Are you so lacking in understanding, also?"* (New American Standard)

Jesus had large congregations listening to His teaching. He taught in the synagogues, and on the hillsides to upwards of five thousand people. He said that He was teaching for the purpose of understanding. Teaching provides an atmosphere that stimulates thinking. It answers the questions of "who" is to do the ministry and "what" they are to do. It is a mental exercise; therefore, it can result in personal change, or in just more knowledge. But it is always the starting point for change.

We are teaching in our churches, in conferences, on videos, in our families, and in our businesses. The church today is not only telling everyone the good news, but we are probably doing a better job of teaching than we have ever done.

Jesus Trained Some To Do The Work

Luke 10:1-2 *"The Lord commissioned seventy other disciples and sent them off in twos as advance parties into every town and district where He intended to go. 'There is a great harvest, but only a few are working in it, which means that you must pray to the Lord of the harvest that He will send out more reapers.'"* (Phillips)

Jesus trained up to seventy people to go out and actually do the work. The process He employed went like this: He told a truth so that they could hear it, He taught them something so that they could understand it, but He trained them so that they could do it. Does that make sense? An old, but true, saying states, "Telling is not teaching. Listening is not learning. You learn to do by doing." In other words, just because we tell something to someone, it doesn't mean we are teaching him. Just because he is listening, it doesn't mean he is learning. People learn to do by doing. Training has to do with doing.

Training provides an atmosphere in which individual change happens in a small group setting. Those involved are emotionally engaged into relationships with others in the training process. To many of you, training means a weekend seminar where you go for a day, or maybe a training seminar during the week. There may be some teaching at those events, but training involves learning how and when one is to do the things that he or she has been taught. It involves actually going and doing.

If a pastor is a teaching pastor, but is not enabling people to be trained by either him or someone else in his church, he is only accomplishing one aspect of what Jesus did. If a pastor is an evangelist and is on the radio and on television and is passing out tracts and telling many people the good news, but is not taking the people to the next step of teaching or the further step of training, then he is not completing what Jesus asked him to do. So, who are you training in your church? Jesus told everyone, He taught many, He trained some.

Notice this, as the size of the group decreases, there is less organization and more opportunity for relationship. When you are **telling** everyone in a large group context, there is no opportunity for personal relationships. If you are **teaching** many, you can teach principles, but can not have a personal relationship with each individual. When you start **training** you have less organization and deeper relationships. Finally, when you go to **one on one** equipping, you have very high relationship and extremely little organization.

We have a problem in our churches' model today because we haven't followed the model of Jesus. We are heavy on organization and large group structures, but we are not heavy on relationships coming through small group training. A friend of mine just today told me that he was in a church situation where the elders met regularly, but they had no strong relationships with each other; therefore, when a crisis came they were organizational but they were not relational. Most problems that you will have in your church will have little to do with the organization or structure; problems will have to do with relationships. The reason why we have relationship problems in our churches is because we are telling everyone, we are teaching many, we are training some, but we are not doing a good job of the last two things, equipping and modeling a personal relationship with God. The fourth thing that Jesus did was that He equipped a few to reproduce.

He Equipped A Few To Reproduce

Mark 14:17 "*Late in the evening, He arrived with the twelve…*"

Mark 14:33 "*He took with Him Peter, James, and John*" (Phillips)

Jesus set the pattern of equipping a very small group, twelve, and spending additional time and effort with only three. Equipping happens, I believe, within a group of one to twelve. Jesus gave us the model of the twelve because you cannot equip a leader in a large group. The Greek word for equipping is first seen in Mark chapter one, and is translated "mending the nets". It means to take something that is not functioning and make it useable. That is what we are trying to do. When we equip a person, we are taking a person from the pew that is not functioning properly and making him to function correctly for God's use. One's will is motivated as he or she learns to make spiritual choices, and the questions of "where?" and "why?" of the spiritual walk are answered in the equipping process. Who are you giving your life to? Who are the people in your inner circle?

As an aside, Jesus not only equipped Peter, James, and John, but they became His most intimate friends. Those are the men He wanted close when His life took its hardest turn, the Garden of Gethsemane. Who are the people in your inner circle? When you approach the storms of life, who will be the people that you turn to? Are there three people that, if you had a crisis in your life, you would immediately call? Are there three people who care for your soul and who would minister to you? It may take you several years of relationships to find the people who will be in an inner circle, but every one of us needs to have a Peter, James, and John in our life. Pray for such people and seek them out. They may be people other than those you are equipping; they may not even live in your city. But find these folks and nurture these relationships.

Let's look at the final thing Jesus did.

Jesus Modeled A Relationship With His Father So That They Would Catch The Vision

Mark 1:35 "*In the early morning, while it was still dark, Jesus got up, left the house, and went away to a secluded place, and was praying there.*" (New American Standard)

Mark 14:35 "*Then He walked forward a little way and flung himself on the ground, praying that, if it was possible, He might not have to face the ordeal. 'Dear Father,' He said, 'all things are possible to you. Please – let me not have to drink this cup. Yet, not what I will, but what you will.'*" (Phillips)

The goal of all spiritual teaching and training and equipping is to enable men and women to walk with Jesus Christ. The focus is not on our mind, not on our emotion or even our will, but it is on our heart motives. When others watch your life, what do they see? Do you let them get close enough to see you as you really are? Jesus allowed the disciples to be close enough to see Him in His moment of crisis so that they could see His relationship with the Father.

If you are a pastor, you're a leader in your church. If you're a leader in the body of Christ, people are watching you live your life. They want to see how you react when things are going well and they watch how you handle life when you go through a crisis.

They watched what Jesus did in the crisis. They watched the relationship between the Father and the Son. Four times in John 17, Jesus' last prayer on behalf of His precious disciples, He prayed "that they may be one". He desired unity for them, and He allowed them to get close enough to Him that they learned by His model. Do you want unity in your church? Be a model of a man whose heart is wholly God's, and He will create unity.

It is easy to say that Jesus was perfect, so of course He wouldn't mind the disciples getting close. But what man among us wants people close enough to see that he is not perfect? God hasn't asked perfection of us. He has only asked for a seeking heart, one that fears the Lord. That heart He will honor, and that heart in a man will bring others closer to God.

The Bible says in Psalm 25, "*Where is the man who fears the Lord? God will teach him how to choose the best, and he shall live within God's circle of blessing and his children shall inherit the Earth. Friendship with God is reserved for those who reverence Him. With them alone, He shares the secrets of his promise."* (Psalm 25: 12-14)   Where is the man who fears the Lord? God will teach him how to choose the best. Are you allowing people to see you choose the best? Are you allowing them to see the heart motives in your life? When others watch your life, what do they see? Do you let them get close enough to see you as you really are?

Peter, Jesus' Consummate Horse

Jesus' strongest horse was very probably Peter. He showed strong horse characteristic from the very first.

- He followed Jesus immediately, without looking back at his old life. Horses are like that. Whatever they are **focused** on is a commitment that they are passionate about.

- Peter was the first to understand and confess that Jesus was the Christ, the Son of the Living God. (Matthew 16:13-20) He had watched closely, thought about what he was seeing and hearing, and made a conclusion confirmed by God in his heart. He was **not afraid to voice** this belief, even if no one around him had the same understanding or belief.

- He was prone to **speaking before thinking**, and was **strongly opinionated** in doing so. His comments at the Mount of Transfiguration were a hysterical example. He just didn't get it, but he had an opinion about an action (of course) and voiced it without thinking. He should have been watching and worshipping, but, no, he was talking. God Almighty shut him up with His own voice declaring His approval of His Son.

- He was a man of **action**, and never one to shy away from a **fight**. Even in the Garden of Gethsemane, it was Peter who reached for a sword to defend Jesus, and in so doing only managed to cut off a man's ear. Jesus, still training His horse, explained to Peter that this event was happening according to God's will.

- The wind having been taken out of Peter's aggressive sails, he followed the "attack" with denial. He wanted to **act fearless**, but was indeed afraid. Horses do try to hide fear, and will do unimaginable things when faced with the collapse of their world.

- After Jesus' resurrection, the Shepherd and the horse were reconciled, and Jesus **commissioned him** to "shepherd his flock" in John 21:15-23. It is interesting that Peter was a horse who became a shepherd. He pastored the New Testament church with humility and God's wisdom, a completely transformed man. This is a current phenomenon as well. Many business leaders worldwide are becoming house church pastors, and finding God's blessing as they work.

- Peter then spoke at Pentecost (Acts 2), during which thousands were added to the church. He spoke with God's power, because he was completely under God's control. He later spoke before the Sanhedrin (Acts 4:1-22), the very group that terrified him enough to deny Christ a short while earlier. Courage now came from God and not himself. And finally, in a somewhat humorous incident (Acts 10), God sent Peter to shepherd another horse, Cornelius. God knew that Cornelius' heart was searching for Him, but Cornelius was a Gentile whom no Jew would approach with the Gospel. So God instructed Peter to go. Still having the feisty horse personality, Peter argued vehemently. So much so that God had to reprimand him, "Do NOT call unclean, what I have called clean!" Peter went.

What steps did Jesus take in the training of Peter?

- **Jesus first called Peter**. He singled him out, and asked him to come and be with him. The same way, you must find the man who God wants you to invest time in, and ask him.

- **Jesus taught him**. He explained painstakingly, over and over again, the things of God. Horses do not often get it the first, or even the second time. Their thoughts are racing so fast that they do not hear everything, so things need to be explained again. They need to be slowed down to listen. You have to remember this when dealing with horses. Try to get quiet time with them. Invite them to go hunting, fishing (they may balk at fishing, but persevere), or to a sporting event with you. Get them away from everyday life. They will hear what you are saying better in such environments. When they become used to really listening to you, you can talk to them anywhere, even at their own offices. But they must learn to actively listen. In their natural state, they just want to interrupt and give their own half-thought-out ideas.

- **Jesus let Peter get close to him personally**, as an intimate friend. Peter could see how Jesus really lived daily with His Father. He was there to watch how Jesus handled crises and people who opposed Him. Jesus not only modeled the life He had for Peter, but He had Peter close by Him to see it. You, as a shepherd, must become that transparent to a few of your horses. It doesn't come naturally or easily, especially to men. But the fact is that you, as a pastor, need such deep friendship as much as the leaders do. It truly is lonely at the top. When you are the person in charge, who do you talk to? A business leader and a pastor are perfectly suited to be confidants to each other.

- **Jesus was infinitely patient.** If Jesus had not been God as well as man, He may have been tempted often to give Peter a boot and forget about him. But He believed in what Peter would become, and He kept with him. Do you believe in what God can make of your horses enough to spend the extra time with them to ensure their training success?

- **Jesus expressed a vision for what Peter would become.** He gave Simon a new name, Peter, and explained the reason. The name was a vision, that Peter would become a rock, and he did. His leadership became a solid foundation for the New Testament church, a baby institution under attack and in need of strength. Such a horse could provide it, under God's direction. Give your trainees a vision for what they can become. Ask God to reveal to you how to direct them, and He will.

- **Jesus praised Peter when appropriate** ("Blessed are you, Peter"), but was not afraid to **chastise him when necessary** ("Get thee behind me, Satan!"). It took a lot of trust for a relationship to survive and thrive on such openness and honesty, but such a relationship can happen when shepherds are willing to engage their life with that of another.

- **Jesus saw some success, but not the finished product.** You may or may not see the end result of what God is doing through your training of horses.

- **Jesus' efforts with Peter produced multiplication of His ministry.** When you invest your life in someone who goes on to produce more ministry, the effect is of multiplication rather than addition. Your own ministry will be enlarged because as your horses become trained, they help you with the sheep, bringing more and more into the fold.

QUESTIONS

1. What will you do?

      Your church is probably doing a good job of telling the good news, and it is probably doing a fairly good job of teaching; you may even be known as a "training church", but will you do what Jesus did? Will you, as a pastor, also equip a few, and model a relationship with the Father, with his Son, Jesus Christ, and with the Holy Spirit within you?

2. How much time do you spend in each of the five areas (telling, teaching, training, equipping, and modeling)?

      Are you willing to rearrange your schedule to accommodate more time spent in equipping? What can you change, eliminate, or delegate to someone else so that you have more time free to equip?

3. Do you really believe in the power of multiplication? Does it make sense that more time spent with fewer people could actually reap more effective ministry than more time spent with the crowds?

"IN FRENZIED EXCITEMENT HE **EATS UP THE GROUND;** HE CANNOT STAND STILL WHEN THE **TRUMPET SOUNDS.**

AT THE BLAST OF THE TRUMPET **HE SNORTS,** 'AHA!' HE CATCHES THE SCENT OF **BATTLE** FROM AFAR."

Job 39:24-25

chapter three

BUILDING BRIDGES

BETWEEN PASTORS AND WORKPLACE LEADERS

Two years ago, I woke up at 2:00 a.m. I was thinking about a talk I was to give to pastors the next day, and God gave me the following vision.

I see an island off the coast. A shepherd is taking care of his sheep on the island. There is a city on the coast. At night, the shepherd stands and watches the lights in the city brightly flickering from one end to the other. The shepherd is a pastor; the lights are leaders from the workplace. God seemed to say to me, "Build a bridge from the island to the city." The bridge appears. Walking to the middle of the bridge is the shepherd from one side, and the leader from the other. They meet and hug, turn and face the city, get down on their knees, and pray together for the transformation of the city. I thought to myself, "When we understand the vision, we will finally see personal transformation, transformation of our cities and our local churches, and together we will see God build His Kingdom."

Christian marketplace leaders, who are also leaders in the community, are very seldom connected to the church and don't understand their responsibility. Pastors don't understand their responsibility to join with these leaders to reach their companies and communities for God.

What would happen if one business leader and his pastor began to pray for their city together, regularly? What if they met once a week, and asked God to give them the names of twelve individuals from their church who they could ask to be in a small group with them? What if they prayed for a month, and then asked those twelve to join them?

Before looking at the steps a pastor can take, there are a few foundational principles that effect how you relate to these "horses".

Four Ways That Leaders Grow Spiritually

I am not talking now about spiritual growth in general. We must understand this, because leaders grow and learn differently than does the normal person in your congregation. I have interviewed spiritually mature leaders for twenty years, and kept track of their responses. When I asked them to list what influenced them most in their growth with God, they gave me the following responses.

- The fourth on the list is the **encouragement of family or friends**.

- The third influence is being in a **small accountability group**. This is a small group that functions over a long period of time. It has within it a core of about three intimate friends who care about their soul, people to whom they would turn in crises, and who would immediately be there for them.

- Number two is a **role model** or an example. Active mentors, passive mentors, and occasional mentors are crucial. Our church society has become one that is too dependent on the idea than you can learn enough in classes. In the workplace, mentoring is again starting to be accepted and normal. For example, it is common to become an apprentice, where one learns to do by doing. Classes cannot teach experience.

- The first and most important influence is **time alone with God**. As you know, the most dangerous position to be in spiritually is to be the leader of a church. When you are just a businessman, like me, people do not expect much of you, but when you become the head of a church or a Christian organization, they expect that you will be "spiritual". In fact, other people think that they are less spiritual than you. If you listen too hard, you might start to believe them.

It is paramount to keep fresh daily time with God. Get a new version of the Bible to read, and add a challenging devotional book to your reading regimen. My all time favorite is "My Utmost For His Highest" by Oswald Chambers. Some folks purchase a new devotional book each year, to get fresh views. Sing or read the words of songs to God in worship and praise. There are so many ways to keep your quiet time with God fresh. Put some thought to it and do it. It is during that time that our dependence on Him is renewed and refreshed. We can give our day, our thoughts, and our actions to Him, and watch as the Holy

Spirit guides with wisdom and strength. We cannot grow without this time.

Do you notice what is not on the list? A large group setting is not listed. In the average church, eighty per cent of the program occurs in a large group setting, and this format is number five or six when looking at ways leaders grow. I encourage you to interview leaders in your own church (without leading their answers), and I think you will find the same. By "leaders in your church", I do not mean someone who holds a position. I mean someone who is dynamically living his or her life for Christ, who is invested in the lives of others to help them grow spiritually, who is a leader in the community and at work. I think you will find that these people were individually mentored, either by someone in a Christian organization outside the church, or by some other individual who took time with them over a period of time. Although there are exceptions, the church is not normally characterized by discipleship, so most of these were discipled outside of the church. This is only because the church did not offer the equipping.

Jesus modeled training His disciples with all four of these growth patterns. As His years on earth came to a close, He spent more and more time just with the twelve and the three. During the last week of His life here, He taught in the Temple, had the Last Supper with the twelve, went to the Garden with them, and brought the three off to the side to be with Him as He prayed in agony to His Father.

There is certainly nothing wrong with organized church programs, but more time should be spent in the small group and mentoring patterns than is now the norm in today's churches.

Jesus' Pattern of Training

People normally learn in four patterns:

1. Listening … Preaching, TV, Radio
2. Observing … as in a son watching his father
3. Applying … discussing in a group and actually doing the activity
4. Mentoring … one on one coaching

The church is doing a good job with number one, listening, but is doing less with the remaining three. Jesus modeled all four of these patterns. When preaching to the masses, they could listen to learn. By taking His disciples off by themselves, He gave them the opportunity to observe as He modeled a spiritual life. By allowing them talking time privately with Him, He afforded them a chance to apply the things they were hearing and seeing. Finally, He mentored Peter one on one, coaching him to become the foundational leader he would someday be. That is how we learn, too. We listen, observe, apply, and get mentored. Horses need all four of the growth phases, and they need someone to lead them and train them.

Four Words For Today

1. **Kingdom** … It's not about us. It's about Him. Matthew 6:10 says, "*your kingdom come, your will be done, on earth as it is in Heaven.*" It isn't about us, or our churches, or our organizations. It is about His Kingdom and His glory. What I am seeing in the workplace is that there are no labels. It doesn't matter what denomination people are from. When a workplace leader gets together in the

community with other believers, it doesn't matter what church they attend. The only question needed is, "Are you a follower of Jesus?"

2. **Relationships** ... God is into relationships. (John 15 and John 17) Do not give your life for an institution or organization, even the best church in the world. Give your life to relationships with individual people.

When you leave your job, the only thing that will last is relationships. A few years ago I attended a picnic. It was organized by former employees as a reunion. I had sold the firm six years before, and had not been there at all for the previous three years. During that time, many of them had moved to new jobs as well. But three years after we had been together as co-workers, one hundred and fifty people came. Some drove from over five hundred miles away to share a picnic for an afternoon. Why? Relationships. They wanted to be with "family". That is what lasts after the work is done.

Into whom are you investing your time to build relationship?

3. **Community** ... (Acts) People today are dying for community. They sit at a computer all day, then come home and sit in front of a television set. They have all sorts of technology, but they are crying out for community. If the church does not supply community, they will search somewhere else.

4. **Transformation** ... 2 Corinthians 5:17, *"Therefore, if anyone is in Christ, he is a new creation; the old has gone, the new has come!"* Romans 12:2 says, *"Do not conform any longer to the pattern of this world, but be transformed by the renewing of your mind."* We are talking here about

transformation of an individual, transformation of segments of society, and transformation of cities.

We love to talk about local churches, but most of the time that the word "church" is used in the New Testament, it is referring to the body of Christ. For example, if a reference is made to "the church in Galatia", it is referring to the body of Christ in Galatia. The people may have met together, or they may have been scattered into little groups meeting in homes secretly. In the Bible, "transformation" refers to three key areas: individuals, cities, and nations. Our local churches tend to focus on individual transformation, most often to the exclusion of the city and nation. Our focus needs to grow and change.

Now, let's finally look at the six things a pastor can do to implement this new paradigm. If these are followed, your local church will multiply its ministry into the marketplace and community. Jesus modeled all of these with the twelve.

Six Steps For Equipping Leaders

#1 – Call them into a personal relationship with you

Mark 1:16-18, "*As He was going along by the Sea of Galilee, He saw Simon and Andrew, the brother of Simon, casting a net in the sea; for they were fishermen. And Jesus said to them, 'Follow Me, and I will make you become fishers of men.' Immediately they left their nets and followed Him*" (New American Standard)

Jesus was not random. He called each of them by name and invited them into a personal, close, "with Him" relationship. The Bible takes great pains to tell us how Jesus called each of His twelve. It was important that He did it this way. A pastor can do this within his church. How do you know which people to call? Pray, and God will show you. As you pray over these people, remember the following:

- Workplace leaders are lonely. The only one lonelier in the church than the workplace leader is the pastor. They have a lot in common with each other; it is true that it is "lonely at the top".

- They have influence in the workplace and in the community. Remember, we are not talking about every leader. We are talking about dynamic movers and shakers who may or may not be leaders in your church.

- You are each intimidated by the other. Workplace leaders are intimidated by the pastor's spirituality, and feel that they can never be as good. After all, the pastor hears from God and can relate God's truth to others, and the workplace leader thinks he could never do that. The pastor is intimidated by the workplace leader's wealth, position, and power. If pastors only realized how pressured and stressed that wealth, position, and power make them!

> My pastor was still intimidated by me when I was losing hundreds of thousands of dollars, because he did not know it. He thought I was powerful; I thought I was failing, and I was worried, and alone in it. We need to stop playing games and become friends. We need to get close to each other

- Invite them out to lunch.

#2 Create an Atmosphere of Understanding With Them

Matthew 15:15-18, *"Peter said to Him, 'Explain the parable to us.' Jesus said, 'Are you still lacking in understanding also? Do you not understand that everything that goes into the mouth passes into the stomach, and is eliminated? But the things that come out of the mouth come from the heart, and those defile the man.'"*

Jesus spent three years, going over lessons time and again, to create understanding in His disciples. It takes time, patience, and repetition. Remember our example in the first chapter of Zac training a horse? Most pastors do not spend as much time and energy with one person in three years as Zac spends to train a horse in thirty days. It is time to change the way we do church, and free the pastor to spend some of his time to use with the horses. But the normal church will be horrified at the thought of the pastor spending his time differently, so here is the plan:

Do it quietly at first. Choose your twelve, meet with them every week or two, and do not make it common knowledge. By the end of three years, when these leaders are having ministry everywhere, your church is growing because of it, and your members are seeing God working, they will buy into it. Try the following:

- Meet "one on one". This is the beginning. Pray over each one. Ask him to lunch. Ask him if he would be willing to be in a small group with you to pray and talk about ministry in the workplace.
- Get three of them to meet on a regular basis to pray and talk
- Start a group of six to twelve people
- Have fun together
- Be transparent
- This will take time, be available and patient
- The rewards will be fantastic. Give yourself three years to see what God will do.

When you have set up a small group, consider the following aspects of it as you plan.

The question: "How may I, as your pastor, help you to minister where God has sovereignly placed you in the workplace?" This question is your motivation for being with them, and it will be amazing to them. No one has offered such a gift to them before.

The Participants: The pastor and six to twelve leaders from the workplace. They do not necessarily need to be leaders at the church. Their level of spiritual maturity may vary greatly.

The Facilitator: The pastor could lead the group at first (not teaching, but asking questions and listening). After thirty days, he should rotate the leadership of the group each week or turn it over to a business leader. Remember, wild stallions will not stay in a group where they have no authority.

When the group meets, the pastor is not in charge; he is the facilitator. Jesus did not always preach. When alone with His twelve, He asked questions. He made them think and talk together to reach conclusions. This is a totally new paradigm, I know, but Jesus used it very successfully. He made His small group of disciples comfortable enough that they could ask questions; they could even embarrass themselves, and it was OK. The end was a small group of trained men who reached their cities and even their world for God.

(For a complete explanation, get my book "Lasting Investments".)

The Focus: The focus is outward, in the marketplace. Ask, "What is God doing where you work daily?"

The Agenda: The agenda is set by the leaders; it is not a curriculum by the pastor. Ask, "What issues are you dealing with at work?" and, "What are the biggest challenges you are facing at work?" Write down their answers. Then help them go to God's Word to see what He has to say about it. At first, they won't trust you, so they won't give you their deepest problems and challenges. But eventually they will trust you and share real stuff, and when they do, you cannot go back to staff meeting and share what John's real problem is. You must keep strong confidences. Assist the group to answer the above questions, and then assist them to help each other have a ministry where they work.

The Resources: The Word of God, the Holy Spirit, Prayer, the leader's creative questions, and the circumstances of daily life are all that is needed.

The Requirement: A heart for God and a desire to join Him in His work.

Don't look for the richest business leader, or the strongest personality. Don't seek the most popular one, or the most gifted one. Look for the one who has a heart for God, and a heart for people. Look for one who seems teachable.

The Commitment: Minimum of six months.

The Time: One hour to an hour and a half, weekly, on a weekday before work.

The Place: A conference room at one of their offices

#3 Affirm Them in Their Workplace Calling

Luke 10:1-4,16 *"Now after this the Lord appointed seventy others, and sent them in pairs ahead of Him to every city and place where He Himself was going to come. And He was saying to them, 'The harvest is plentiful, but the laborers are few; therefore, beseech the Lord of the harvest to send out laborers into His harvest. Go; behold, I send you out as lambs in the midst of wolves… The one who listens to you listens to Me, and the one who rejects you rejects Me; and he who rejects Me rejects the One who sent Me.'"*

- If you, as a pastor, do not affirm the laborers, who will? Most church members in the pew do not realize that they are to be ministers out in their neighborhoods and workplaces. They think they are paying you to do the work of the ministry. They feel like "second class citizens" spiritually, because they look at someone on the platform and say to themselves, "I could never do that. I'll just sit here and listen. Then I will go home, then I will go to work. Next Sunday, I'll come back again. That's all there is to it."

- Normally, they live segmented lives, in which what they do and say on Sunday has little bearing on how they run their business on Tuesday afternoon. Therefore, we have to teach and train them to have integrated lives. They need to know that all of it, their job, family, money, leisure, church, and community is all about Jesus. Let them see you up close to see how this is done.

- Many of them are on the spiritual sidelines of ministry. They need to realize that the power of the risen Christ dwells in them, and see what that means in everyday life. They need to know that ministry is the calling, ministry is the privilege, and ministry is the responsibility of every member of the body of Christ. When they understand this, we can equip them to be sensitive to the lost, to listen to the lost, to share the good news, to serve and not be served, and be prepared for battle. We need to send them out and to join them as they go out.

> Henry Blackaby tells the story about a time when he was in Canada. He had a small church and he visited every member of his church in

their workplace to find out what they were facing there. I would ask you, "When was the last time that you visited leaders at their workplace, to see how you could serve them and equip them in their workplace?" I am convinced that if we could get our pastors out of their studies, out of their offices, out of the church buildings, and into the community to work with their members, we would do church differently. Go with them to their Jerusalem, and to their Judah; visit their offices, their schools, and their factories. Go with them as they go outside the walls of their church so that your walls are extended.

They are called to join God where he is working out in their world, not necessarily to join the ministry that God has given you. There is a difference. The goal is to build them up with a Kingdom focus, not to build our own church, or our own ministry, or ourselves. Richard Halverson said, "The focus must be where we are between Sundays." The truth is that the church will grow automatically when a Kingdom focus is being exercised by your church members.

- Get Them Started. Matthew 20:6-7 *"And about the eleventh hour he went out and found others standing around; and he said to them, 'Why have you been standing here idle all day long?' They said to him, 'Because no one hired us.' He said to them, 'You go into the vineyard, too.'"*

Many people are standing on the sidelines of ministry, not realizing that they have been hired, and not knowing what to do. Affirm them in their calling, and ask them, "How may I help you in your ministry in the place where God has sovereignly placed you?" This question is the most important question that you can ask. It alone will transform your ministry.

#4 Equip Them as Ministers in The Workplace

Ephesians 4:11-13 *"And He gave some as apostles, and some as prophets, and some as evangelists, and some as pastors and teachers, for the equipping of the saints for the work of service, to the building up of the body of Christ; until we all attain to the unity of the faith, and of the knowledge of the Son of God, to a mature man, to the measure of the stature which belongs to the fullness of Christ."*

- Get to know what situations they are facing in the workplace, home, and community.

- Pray with them over those situations and opportunities.

- Strategize with them as to how to use these opportunities. It is possible that your willingness to do this will surprise them. Ask them, "What is God speaking to *you* about? What do you want to see happen at work?" Then help them come up with a plan.

- Teach them the difference in "Church Work" and the "Work of the Church".

   Church Work is draining for horses. They don't feel fulfilled with it or see the vision for it. But the Work of the Church is to bring people to Christ and see them grow to maturity. Horses get excited about that. Horses need a big vision, one that encompasses the whole community, the country, even the world. Don't give small vision – Jesus didn't.

#5 Commission Them as World Ambassadors for Christ

Matthew 28:18-20 *"And Jesus came up and spoke to them, saying, 'All authority has been given to Me in Heaven and on earth. Go, therefore, and make disciples of all nations, baptizing them in the name of the Father and the Son and the Holy Spirit, teaching them to observe all that I have commanded you; and lo, I am with you always, even to the end of the age.' "*

- Commission them publicly, in front of the church. Lay hands on them and pray over them, and commission them as full-time ministers of the Gospel. Churches do this when sending missionaries to another country. Well, these horses are missionaries in another 'country', their workplaces and communities. If you commission them like they were a missionary, they will feel like a missionary. Let them sense the anointing of the Holy Spirit.

- Commission a different group each month – teachers, government employees, retail personnel, financial workers, high tech employees, etc.

Isn't it interesting that it does not cost your church any money to send out these missionaries? They can go places even missionaries can't go, such as China. Not only can they go as marketplace people, but their secular companies pay for this mission activity!

#6 Release Them for Service in Their Own Sphere of Influence

Acts 1:8 *"but you will receive power when the Holy Spirit has come upon you; and you shall be My witnesses both in Jerusalem, and in all Judea, and Samaria, and even to the remotest part of the earth."*

- Release them. This is the hardest part for the pastor. That means you have to give up control. You can't count it, number it, or put your name on it. You release them into their world, and allow God to get all the glory.

- They should be equipping others after six months to three years.

- Remember, ministry in the workplace takes time, patience, and creativity.

- Continue to pray for them, even when you do not see immediate results.

- Bring them together with their peers for further equipping and encouragement.

- Have them give reports in your services about what is happening in the workplace. The local church has now become an equipping and sending station for the battle. I agree with George Barna, who, in his book *Revolution* said, "Love the revolutionaries in your midst and remember that they are disciples who seek God with all of their heart, mind, strength, and soul."[1]

QUESTIONS

1. *Are you ready to begin?*

    Have you prayed over a few names?

2. *Have you cleared some time in your schedule?*

    Try to have one lunch per week until you have found your small group.

3. *Have you considered asking another pastor to do this in his church, also, so that you can have companionship in this new endeavor?*

    It is always helpful to have another person for question asking and brain-storming.

---

1. George Barna, *Revolution* (Wheaton, IL.: Tyndale, 2005), 140.

CONCLUSION

I challenge you to read the Gospels several times over the next few weeks. See for yourself what Jesus did and how He related to the twelve disciples that He recruited from the marketplace. Watch closely to see exactly how Jesus trained and equipped this band of wild horses to become the leaders of the early church. Notice the transformation of Peter, James, John, and the others. Ask the Holy Spirit to give you the courage to start on this new journey.

This transformation will not occur overnight; however, I promise you that as you begin to shepherd your horses, following the example of the Great Shepherd, and building bridges of relationship, God will bless and multiply your efforts. Your ministry will be deepened and His Kingdom will be expanded.

We stand ready to serve you.

Kent Humphreys

Philemon 1:7   *"Your love has given me great joy and encouragement, because you, brother, have refreshed the hearts of the saints."*

HOW MAY WE HELP YOU?

I would like to offer my services to you. Please feel free to go to:

www.christatwork.com or www.fcci.org.

Click on the link to "The Pastor's Study" for helps and materials.

(Christ @ Work equips and encourages business leaders across the United States and around the world. Their vision is, "Transforming the world, through Christ, one company leader at a time." They have thirty years of resources to help you in understanding the move of God in the workplace.)

You may contact me personally by e-mailing
kent@fcci.org   khumphreys@ahpartners.com

or visit our website,
www.lifestyleimpact.com

Shepherding Horses, Understanding
God's Plan for Transforming Leaders
Published by DiaKonia Publishing
PO Box 9512
Greensboro, NC 27629-0512

www.ephesians412.net